The Brain Workout: 10 Brain Exercises to Help you Start Thinking Like a BOSS

Many times we are asked how we began our journey to becoming our own BOSS or starting our own business. Our response to that is you have to learn how to exercise your brain to think like a BOSS. Our definition of a BOSS is a successful leader who has properly trained their brain to move forward and upward to achieve goals. We all know that in order to get results from the gym you have to commit yourself to going; similarly, if you want to become a BOSS you have to commit to take the necessary actions to become one. In this guide we will cover how to exercise your brain to think like a BOSS and to ultimately become ONE.

This guide was authored by Robert and Tammira Lucas to help individuals develop a mindset that will allow them to follow their dreams of becoming their own BOSS.

Exercise 1: Train Your Brain to Set Goals

Successful Leaders Have a Target and Goals- They understand there is one fundamental in life: understanding where you are aiming so that you can start shooting towards it. The target is your goal and the shot is your actions toward that target.

Think S.M.A.R.T- Create Goals that are Specific, Measurable, Achievable, Relevant and Timely. (See worksheet 1)

See the Vision- A great way to set goals is to begin with yearly goals. Create a vision board of your goals for the year. You can set your board in four quadrants to represent each quarter of the year. This will allow you to see your goals, not only for the year, but quarterly as well. Display this board where you will see it everyday. Seeing your goals helps you to stay on target. You should also do a board with long-term goals 5 years out.

Being a BOSS, you have to know exactly what you want out of life, where you want to be and what your purpose is. Your actions speak louder than your words — and if you are chasing success, there is nothing that will stop YOU.

"Whatever the mind of man can conceive and believe, it can achieve."

-Napoleon Hill

Exercise Activity #1 SMART Goal (Worksheet1)

Today's Date: _____ Target Date: _____
Start Date: _____

Date Achieved: _____

Goal:
_____
_____

Verify that your goal is SMART

Specific: *What exactly will you accomplish?*

_____
_____
_____
_____

Measurable: *How will you know when you have reached this goal?*

_____
_____
_____

Achievable: *Is achieving this goal realistic with effort and commitment? Do you have the resources to achieve this goal? If not, how will you get them?*

_____
_____

Relevant: *Why is this goal significant to your life?*
_____
_____

Timely: *When will you achieve this goal?*
_____
_____
_____

This goal is important because:
_____
_____
_____

The benefits of achieving this goal will be:
_____
_____
_____

Take Action!

Potential Obstacles	Potential Solutions
_____	_____
_____	_____
_____	_____
_____	_____

Who are the people you will ask to help you?

_____

_____

_____

Specific Action Steps: *What steps need to be taken to get you to your goal?*

What?	Expected Completion Date	Completed
_____	_____	☐
_____	_____	☐
_____	_____	☐
_____	_____	☐
_____	_____	☐

Exercise 2: Thinking Positive

Successful Leaders Are Positive Thinkers- They look at life through rose-colored lenses, optimistically and strongly holding on to their vision, even in the midst of adversity. Successful leaders believe that they have the ability to do anything they set their minds to and eventually do so. They are ambitious and believe that they can conquer any obstacle using their strong will power as an internal motivator.

Create affirmations to help you think positively. *Positive affirmations* are positive declarations that engage the mind to new truths and beliefs. They conquer and change previous erroneous patterns and beliefs when supported by ongoing self-reinforcement. As positive beliefs and truths are realized into the subconscious, one will experience life with less effort and an increased energy level.

Your affirmations should not be general. They should be detailed to include what you are trying to accomplish. Say these affirmations at the start of every day and it will help you to overcome any negative thoughts or feelings.

Write and say your affirmations every day. We suggest posting them on a wall in your house or even your refrigerator. One of the things my husband and I do as a couple before we leave out of the house is say our affirmations as we are walking out the door. As you recite them, be conscious to attach a positive feeling or state to the affirmation as you think, write, or say it. Practice not allowing negative thoughts or emotions to interrupt the positive flow. Trust the process of the power of your mind.

Robert's Technique

As an entrepreneur I've learned that in order to be positive you have to surround yourself around positive people. I always see the positive in every situation, because I know that everything happens for a reason. My quote to reinforce this mindset is, "You never lose, you either win or you learn."

Notes

"The Only way to Predict the Future is to Create IT"

-Peter Drucker

Exercise Activity #2

Keep a log for one week. Write down 10 great things that happen each day. Include even the small things like: *Someone held the door open for me; I found a quarter on the sidewalk; when I went shopping, the clerk at the store was really friendly and helpful.* This activity will help you focus on the positive and evaluate your feelings during the week.

The Positive Focus

	Positive Things	Negative Things
Sunday	1. 2. 3. 4. 5.	1. 2. 3. 4. 5
Monday	1. 2. 3. 4. 5.	1. 2. 3. 4. 5.
Tuesday	1. 2. 3. 4. 5.	1. 2. 3. 4. 5.
Wednesday	1. 2. 3. 4. 5.	1. 2. 3. 4. 5.
Thursday	1. 2. 3. 4. 5.	1. 2. 3. 4. 5.
Friday	1. 2. 3. 4. 5.	1. 2. 3. 4. 5.
Saturday	1. 2. 3. 4. 5.	1. 2. 3. 4. 5.

The Positive Focus Cont.

	Positive Things	Negative Things
Sunday	6. 7. 8. 9. 10.	6. 7. 8. 9. 10.
Monday	6. 7. 8. 9. 10.	6. 7. 8. 9. 10.
Tuesday	6. 7. 8. 9. 10.	6. 7. 8. 9. 10.
Wednesday	6. 7. 8. 9. 10.	6. 7. 8. 9. 10.
Thursday	6. 7. 8. 9. 10.	6. 7. 8. 9. 10.
Friday	6. 7. 8. 9. 10.	6. 7. 8. 9. 10.
Saturday	6. 7. 8. 9. 10.	6. 7. 8. 9. 10.

"A Positive Mind is a Powerful Mind"

"The only person you are destined to become is the person you decide to be."
–Ralph Waldo Emerson

Exercise 3: Growth Mindset

Successful Leaders Love Innovation and Change: They are always thinking about what is on the horizon, and not what is right in front of them. They welcome risks into their lives and are okay with sacrificing and risking it all for the greater good of their goal. They understand that risk and chance gives us the opportunity to evolve, and allows us to conquer and triumph against any adversity. This mindset demands that Successful Leaders stay on the cusp of an ever-changing world.

In the world of business you have to think for the future and longevity. It is important that you learn to think outside of the box and not follow the trends of others. What will take you to the next level? What are others NOT doing that you know you will be good at doing? It is very important to set yourself aside from the competition.

Attend seminars, workshops, classes etc. to help you learn new things. The BOSS that is always learning is a BOSS that is successful. Understand that everything in life is about experience and the day you stop learning is the day you are dead. You should always ask questions and look to further your knowledge.

Refer to your goal list often. This list should be reachable at all times. Create a quarterly schedule of workshops and seminars that are useful to help you or your business grow. Think outside of the box of common seminars that you may attend such as Marketing, finance etc. One of the cool things I did for my business was attended The Bronner Brothers Hair Show. Many would think this was for pleasure, but we accomplished two things on this trip: business seminars and networking with various vendors.

Notes

Exercise 4: Use Daily Challenges as Learning Opportunities

Look at challenges as exciting rather than threatening. Challenges are good and you should think of them as learning opportunities. The experience will help you to better yourself. We as humans are our own biggest critics. Understand that everything will not be perfect and there will always be challenges. You have to recognize that you are only as great as you tell yourself you are. It is human nature for you to feel upset when challenges arise, but it is very important to learn how to overcome these challenges in a short time period. I don't spend more than 10 minutes being upset with a challenge. I immediately begin to think strategically as to how I can change the present to move on to the future.

Tammira's Technique

Each day as a family we sit at the dinner table and we talk about the highs and lows of our day. This gives us an opportunity to hear about each other's day and also offer advice on how we could have taken a challenge in the day and turn it into a triumph. We never dwell on the obstacles.

"You Either Win or you Learn"

"It's fine to celebrate success but it is more important to heed the lessons of failure."
-Bill Gates

Exercise 5: Visualize Your Future

The saying, "If you believe it you will achieve it" is a true statement. Researchers have found that your brain sees no difference between visualizing something and actually doing it. Take some time each day and visualize what you want for your future. When you visualize, it activates the creative powers of your subconscious mind. Jack Canfield said it best, "When you visualize your goals as already complete each and every day, it creates a conflict in your subconscious mind between what you are visualizing and what you currently have. Through the powers of your imagination, you can visualize your future."

The process for visualization only requires you to close your eyes and see yourself as you would be if your goal was completed, received or accomplished. Your visualization should be as clear as possible.

Your subconscious mind will work to create the picture or mental image in your mind, which means you want to determine exactly what it is that you want and then convey the detailed description through visualization.

So you are opening your own kids' boutique. *What does it look like? What color is the paint on the walls? What does the displays look like? What does the employees look like? What type of clothing will be in the store? Will you offer various services?*

Now that you know exactly what your boutique looks like, you can add sensory details to increase the impact your visualization has on your subconscious mind. Think about adding smells, tastes, sounds and feelings. If your boutique carries kids' fragrances, lip gloss or lotions or even bubble bath, *what are the scents that you would smell in your store?*

After you have visualized all the details of the store, now attach a positive emotion to it. Emotions give our visualizations energy. They are what propel your vision forward. Imagine the pride and happiness that comes with ownership of your store. Imagine the satisfaction of achieving your goal.

How happy are you to go to work each day for yourself? Feel the excitement of finally being able to do something that you love. Feel the emotions as intensely as possible for this will help to lock the image in your memory.

Tammira's Visualization Technique

I sit with my eyes closed for about 20 minutes a day and simply visualize my future. I write each of my goals down and review, **affirm** and visualize them daily. This is the most vital thing you can do to turn your dreams in to reality.

Notes

Exercise 6: A Creative Mind Equals a Powerful Mind

Creativity is a mental and social process involving the generation of new ideas or concepts, or new associations of the creative mind between existing ideas or concepts. The process of either conscious or unconscious insight fuels creativity. Training the mind to become more creative can only be done through practice.

Identify where you do your best thinking that allows you to come up with creative ideas. *Is it in the car? In the Shower? Or when you are simply laying down for bed? What time of day is it? The morning? Noon? Or Night?* Some of the best ideas may come to you at the craziest time.

But you want to ensure that you are prepared. Carry a pen and pad or utilize your phone to jot your thoughts. Using your imagination gives you the ability to create in your mind beyond your present reality. Practice the art of using your creative imagination by experimenting with a few of your ideas. You will never know until you try!

Robert's Creative mind Technique

My most creative thoughts come when I am in a place of serenity. This normally occurs late at night after I have come from the gym and showered. I put on my robe, and make my way to my man cave, alone. I get in my favorite recliner with my laptop and allow my creative thoughts to flow.

"You can't use up creativity. The more you use, the more you have."
–Maya Angelou

Exercise 7: Risk + Sacrifice = Success

To risk nothing is to gain nothing. We tend to view risk-taking negatively, often regarding it as dangerous and even unwise. In the business world any BOSS will tell you, the greater the risk, the greater the room for gains and growth. While some risks certainly don't pay off, it's important to remember that some do. Think of risks as an opportunity to succeed rather than a path to failure.

So, what are the opportunities in risk taking? Taking a risk gives you the opportunity to stand out as a leader, rather than a follower that is satisfied with the status quo. *How many times have you taken a risk and the results were greater than you could have expected? Didn't you feel awesome?* Beyond the external opportunities and recognition that risk-taking can bring, it also provides an opportunity for internal growth.

Taking risks is necessary in actively pursuing success whether it is personally or professionally. It can benefit your career-path and create great opportunities for you. As you prepare yourself to take risks, ensure that you have educated and prepared yourself for ALL the possibilities. Prepare the "Pros" and "Cons" of the risk. Understand that all risk may not turn out as you anticipate, but in order to grow you must have the courage to step out from the crowd. You have to break through the limitations that restrict your mind to the life that you are living right now!

Robert's Technique

I always educate myself on the market that I am tapping into. I never make an investment or decision without researching thoroughly. I understand that sacrifice plays an important role in succeeding. Whatever I believe in, I know I have to be willing to put it all on the line. I am fearless when it comes to succeeding.

"Change your thoughts and you change your world."
–Norman Vincent Peale

Notes

Exercise 8: Feed Your Brain with Knowledge

People who engage in physical exercise first thing in the morning have been shown to be brighter, more creative, and more intelligent throughout the day. This applies to feeding your brain with knowledge. It is said that those that consistently look for resources to help themselves grow are more productive in their career.

Reading is very important when you want to THINK like a BOSS. If you do the research, you will find that many of your favorite successful leaders, most if not all, will explain how reading played a huge role in their success. You should spend at least 2-3 hours a day reading or stimulating your brain with knowledge and positivity. Each quarter purchase a new set of 4 to 6 books that will help you stimulate your mind and increase your knowledge.

Technology is so amazing these days that it makes reading or obtaining knowledge easier than ever. Subscribe to your favorite blog. You will be amazed at the wealth of knowledge you can find on a blog. The creation of IPods, IPads and IPhones gives us the ability to listen to books during the course of the day. They also allow us to purchase eBooks, which maybe be more convenient for some. Whether you choose paper or electronic, you always want to ensure you are stimulating your mind with as much knowledge as possible. Here is one way to kill two birds with one stone, while you are working out your body, work out your brain and put your favorite motivational speaker CD or podcast on and listen to it.

Reading makes us more creative and helps us believe that new ideas can become reality. A well-written book or book summary that offers you a pearl of wisdom sparks your creativity, or puts a skip back into your step is worth an investment of at least 1 to 2 hours each day.

So what are some books The Lucas' suggests to help you start thinking like a BOSS?

1. The Success Principles, Jack Canfield
2. Say It Like Obama and Win, Shel Leanne
3. Think and Grow Rich, Napoleon Hill
4. Wooden on Leadership, John Wooden
5. No Excuses, Brian Tracey
6. Black Business Secrets, Dante Lee
7. Daily Motivations for African-American Success, Dennis Kimbro
8. 168 Hours: You Have More Time Than You Think, Laura Vanderkam

Tammira's Technique

I use reading time as a time to bond with myself. I find so much exciting information in a book, blog, and newspapers. Each day I set a specific time at night to read and fill my mind with knowledge.

"The only way of finding the limits of the possible is by going beyond them into the impossible."

–Arthur C. Clarke

Exercise 9: "Focus-to-Finish" Mindset

Successful people have the same list of tasks to accomplish as anyone else. The difference however, is that they make time to get them all done with no excuses. The goals that you set should always be goals that you accomplish. In other words, WHAT YOU START, YOU FINISH! Don't be a part of the trend of setting yearly goals in the New Year and not finishing them. You never want to leave things undone or left in the atmosphere.

If you are setting goals (daily, weekly, monthly, yearly), you should have a date set to when you want those goals accomplished. When you create your task list in Exercise Activity 1, you want to ensure that you complete each task YOU have identified. DO NOT start a task and never finish it! That's like a person cutting half your hair and not finishing. Don't walk around with a half cut head!!

When you set in your mind that you will not start a new task until you've finished what you are working on, it motivates you to complete the task at hand. Visualize the satisfaction of jumping the hurdle in front of you, and also recognize that you have other hurdles (goals and objective) to meet before you reach the finish line. This is where multi-tasking can be your enemy if you attempt to rush the process. Many people try to do too much at one time that they NEVER complete any task. Only multi-task when you are able to complete all tasks you are working on at the same time.

Here are some suggestions when focusing your mind to finish:

1. Determine what your short-term and/or long-term goals are.
2. Create a plan on how these goals need to be accomplished.
3. Create a task list that will help you achieve those goals.
4. Ensure that you are setting dates of completion for each task identified.
5. FINISH each task!

Robert's Technique:

I am not good at multi-tasking, so I avoid doing more than one task at a time. I always ensure that I complete a task before I move on and it always gives me a great feeling of completion.

"You can never cross the ocean until you have the courage to lose sight of the shore."
–Christopher Columbus

Exercise 10: BELIEVE In Your Dreams

What is a dream if you don't actually believe it can happen? How can anyone else believe in your vision if you don't if you don't truly believe it? Everything begins in the heart and mind. Every great achievement begins in the mind of one person. Being a BOSS requires you to be passionate about your goals and passionate about achieving them. How many times have you worked for a company but could care less about how the results of your work will impact others? Probably often because you aren't or weren't passionate about what it is you were doing. You did not believe that this work could potentially help you achieve your dreams. Remember earlier in the guide we stated that your brain does not know the difference between you visualizing something, than you actually doing it.

So let's take an example from me Tammira. When I was younger I would always dream of me being my own boss. I would sit for hours and just think of how my company would run, who would be in my company and how lucrative it would be. As I got older and begin working for various companies and organizations I would always study the top management and how they worked and interact with their employees. I would always tell my colleagues that the work I was currently doing I would not be doing for long because I belong at the top! They thought I was crazy and too ambitious. I set a date on when my last day with the company would be and I would actually leave that day. When I first set the date people would ask me where am I going, and my response would be "I don't know but I have gotten all I need here and it is time for me to depart."

The point of this example is that no matter what others believed, I believed in my dreams, my future and goals. I took the necessary actions to achieve them because just dreaming about them will not make them come true. Understand that when you are passionate, persistent, and know your purpose, you will be able to achieve anything you set your mind too. Always remember, *"The Sky is not the Limit, it's just the Beginning."*

Here are some tips to staying Focus:

1. **Read more. It's really fundamental more than we think!** Reading tests your mind's ability to stay focused on just one task at a time and can improve your focus. Reading helps stimulate your brain!
2. **Burn those procrastination habits.** Procrastination is the thief of time. Avoid delaying any of your activities by leaving things to be done for tomorrow, next week, or next month. Remember that To-do list we talked about, STICK to it!
3. **Multi-tasking is not always a good idea.** You may think that multi-tasking is great because it allows you to accomplish a variety of tasks at once, but you're wrong. Multi-tasking actually confuses your brain and slows you down, keeping you from being fully engaged in any one task. Take it one task at a time and always put the biggest or daunting task first!
4. **Avoid those awful distractions.** Distractions are the enemies of focus. Turn off the phone; don't login in to G-chat; no Facebook or Instagram breaks. All the things you find yourself doing in the middle of a task, AVOID!

> "If you can dream it, you can achieve it."
> –Zig Ziglar

Notes

To learn more information about Tammira Lucas and her coaching systems visit her website at www.tammiralcuas.com or email her at info@tammiralucas.com

www.ingramcontent.com/pod-product-compliance
Lightning Source LLC
Chambersburg PA
CBHW070720180526
45167CB00004B/1557